Speaking From Experience
Dennis J. Murphy

Increasing EMPLOYEE MOTIVATION
A Guide for Supervisors

Professional Training
Associates, Inc.

210 Commerce Boulevard
Round Rock, TX 78664-2189
(512) 255-6006

ISBN 1-877948-05-5

INTRODUCTIONS

The Series

The "Speaking From Experience" series is an effort to put into your hands the ideas, the techniques and the philosophy of effective supervision. This is a series based on the experience and feedback we've received as we travel throughout the country presenting seminars for working supervisors. We offer you the ideas and practices that are actually used in successful organizations, including our own. We've found that there are really no secret formulas for success in a business or for success in working with people. Most of the ideas and practices that work come not from theory or inspiration, but rather from experience.

Learning from experience means learning from both successes and mistakes. This series is an attempt to share what other successful supervisors have already learned. We hope you will find in these pages ideas that make it possible for you to arrive at your own goals a little sooner and to get more enjoyment out of the work as you move toward your own goals. We spend many hours working; in fact, most of us spend the majority of our waking hours at work. As much as possible, one ought to be able to enjoy that work and feel that the efforts are productive and successful.

Increasing Employee Motivation

"Increasing Employee Motivation" is one of three titles in the "Speaking From Experience" series. The other titles are "Successful Time Management" and "Effective Supervision: A Handbook." This book on motivation stresses that supervisors can influence employees with practical steps and ACTION rather than theory. It is written with the working supervisor in mind. It can be read from cover to cover or a section at a time. Pick it up and start where you like. Don't overlook the checklists and planning pages in the back.

The Author

Dennis J. Murphy is an optimist, a skeptic, and a realist. He has an ever-enduring faith in people, an uncurable optimism about getting cooperation from employees, and at the same time, the realistic approach that comes with experience. He understands the supervisor's point of view.

Dennis Murphy has conducted seminars for over 5,000 supervisors. He has worked with supervisors and foremen from coal mines, the aerospace industry, the oil industry, publishing companies, hospitals, and community action groups.

Dennis Murphy has a B.A. in Business from St. Ambrose College and an M.A. in Social Work from the University of Iowa, but feels that the real credentials for writing a book on supervision are his own experiences as a supervisor and his contacts with supervisors all over the United States.

CONTENTS

UP FRONT

This is a book on motivation with practical, up-to-date information for supervisors. We have done seminars all over the United States and talked with thousands of supervisors. We understand that a supervisor is faced every day with problems that require instant, on-the-spot decisions. We also know that most supervisors come to their jobs with excellent work skills, a fairly good sense of what it takes to work with people, but with very little formal training in supervision. In this book you will find very helpful ideas about motivating employees based on our experience with supervisors. You'll find very little discussion of formal theory, as **we believe that supervisors want practical ideas, not theoretical discussions.**

We know that supervisors need a basic working approach to motivation; and that it doesn't help to present gimmicks, or to promise that employees can be motivated overnight. Our recommendations to supervisors who want to improve employee performance include the following steps:

1.
ASK FOR PERFORMANCE. In our seminars, we regularly are asked the question, "How do I motivate my employees?" Sometimes the question is, "How do I motivate younger employees?" or, "How do I motivate older employees?" Sometimes the question is, "How do I motivate engineers, or artists, or secretaries, or social workers?" No matter who you are trying to motivate, there is another question to be asked first, **"What do I want the employee to do, that he or she is not doing now?"** You need to know exactly what you want the employee to do. You should be able to describe what is being done now, and be able to tell the employee how you want the performance to change.

2.
LEARN WHAT WORKS. If you want to change what someone else is doing, it helps to have a general idea about the kinds of things that motivate people to work, and to know under what conditions employees are most likely to cooperate and to follow instructions. When you get down to actual cases, you will find employees can be very different and yet it's our experience that successful supervisors across the country use many of the same approaches to a wide variety of employees. In the section of the book titled, Motivators That Work, you'll find some ideas about the motivators supervisors can use. For example, there is a discussion of why, **from a supervisor's point of view, self-esteem is a much stronger motivator than wages.**

3. BUILD RELATIONSHIPS. Supervision is a people business. **If supervisors want to motivate employees, they need to establish and maintain relationships with employees that are based on trust, fairness and consistency.** We know that this is not always easy; particularly in work situations where there are labor-management problems. What we know from our experience is that there are supervisors who manage to maintain a good trusting relationship even in very adverse situations. In our seminars, we often have a very interesting discussion about whether or not it is possible to be honest with employees. While honesty seems to be a good idea to most supervisors, a number of them find themselves in situations where they are not comfortable sharing information with employees. Some supervisors tell us that they think it is a good idea to tell "white lies," or distort information slightly as a way of motivating employees. For example, they might threaten dismissal when they know that they would not actually fire an employee for a particular offense. While we understand the dilemmas that supervisors face, **we feel that honesty is the best, and in fact, the only policy for a supervisor.** In our section on Trust, we will offer some guidelines and some ways of resolving the very real dilemmas that supervisors face in regard to honesty.

4. MOTIVATE YOURSELF. The supervisors who are good at motivating employees are also the ones who are continually motivating themselves. They provide a model for employees by meeting their own goals, using their time efficiently, and approaching their work with a sense of urgency. **They convey to employees that it really does matter whether the work gets finished on time, and that quality and deadlines are important.** An interesting discovery as we talk to supervisors across the nation is that the nature of the work itself doesn't necessarily determine whether workers will be motivated. It's a little surprising to find workers in jobs that look appealing, artists, engineers, executives, even celebrities, who tell us that their jobs become boring after awhile, and that it is hard to be enthusiastic about their work. What's even more surprising is to find people doing jobs that appear boring and adverse who are having a great time doing their work. In every case where we found people enjoying what looked like a terrible job, we also found a supervisor who was a good motivator.

5. CREATE A PRODUCTIVE CLIMATE. Every organization has a distinct climate or working atmosphere. As we travel throughout the country visiting organizations, we've become adept at quickly assessing the work climate. We pay attention to the way people greet each other. We're interested in whether employees are comfortable in asking questions of their supervisors. We notice how buildings and grounds are kept.

A good supervisor should be able to assess the work climate in his own organization and be aware of his own contribution to that climate. **The relationship between supervisor and employees is so important that it often sets the tone for the entire department.** We've included some ideas about how to assess the work climate and also some tips for the supervisor who wants to improve the working atmosphere.

6. **WALK IN THEIR SHOES.** An essential part of motivating employees is understanding the employee's point of view. A supervisor needs input from his or her employees and the ability to use that input in resolving performance problems. **A common mistake supervisors make is to give direction and advice without first listening to employees.** Sometimes it seems as if listening to employees or taking time to hear their side of the story means that we are agreeing with them or giving in. In actual practice, hearing someone out as they discuss their concerns conveys the feeling that the ideas are important. When we listen first, employees are more cooperative.

7. **REFUSE TO ACCEPT POOR PERFORMANCE.** A topic you don't see much about in books on "motivation" is reprimands. The fact is that supervisors do have to tell employees when their performance is not acceptable. Sometimes this feedback takes the form of a reprimand. We will be sharing some ideas about reprimands including a format you can use to effectively reprimand, and still allow the employee to maintain a sense of dignity and self-esteem. **One of the keys to an effective reprimand is to reassure the employee that in the other areas of their work, their performance is still acceptable and appreciated.**

8. **DEVELOP YOUR OWN POWER.** In this book, you will also find a section on Power. Supervisors need to develop and refine their own sense of personal power. We present here some ideas about how to effectively use your own power without appearing to be constantly ready to do battle. **Personal power used effectively is more like a gentle wind moving a huge sailboat than like a sledge hammer breaking rock.**

9. **BUILD TEAMWORK.** We've concluded our book with a discussion of quality circles. Quality circles were developed in Japan, and we are now finding that they can also help American industries to improve productivity. Ours is a general discussion which points out some of the key benefits of this approach and includes ideas that individual supervisors can use even when their management isn't interested in the formal Quality Circle Program.

We hope you will find helpful ideas on these pages. By our definition, **an idea is helpful only if after reading the book,** you change your approach to an employee and if your new approach results in improved employee performance.

ASK FOR PERFORMANCE

Here's a conversation that occurred between me and a supervisor at a seminar not long ago.

Supervisor: "Can you tell me how to get more work out of my younger employees?"

Me: "I'll sure try. What's the problem?"

Supervisor: "Well, they don't seem to be motivated."

Me: "Not motivated? What do you want them to do that they are not doing now?"

Supervisor: "I'd like them to put out more effort."

Me: "You don't think they are working hard enough?"

Supervisor: "No, they just don't seem to care."

Me: "I'm still not sure what you mean."

Supervisor: "Well, the problem is that they are all so young and they don't know how to work. They think the world owes them a living."

Me: "What do you want them to do that they are not doing now?"

Supervisor: "I'd like them to be more responsible for their work."

Me: "What do you mean 'responsible?'"

Supervisor: "I know they don't care, because they turn their work in with mistakes."

Me: "Do the older, more experienced workers turn in work with mistakes?"

Supervisor: "Yes."

Me: "What's the difference?"

Supervisor: "The young ones have too many mistakes."

Me: "How many is too many?"

Supervisor: "Well, that's hard to say. These are typed reports, and it depends on who they are sent out to."

Me: "On some reports, one mistake is too many?"

Supervisor: "Yes."

Me: "On others, five might be okay?"

Supervisor: "Yes, sometimes."

Notice how even though there have been several questions asked, we haven't talked at all yet about being young and thinking that the world owes them a living as the reasons for not getting the work done.

Whenever you try to motivate someone to do something, be sure you are absolutely clear about what you want before you try to figure out why you are not getting it. Many times, the reason that we don't get what we want is that the expectations have not been made clear to the employee.

In the sample above, the supervisor honestly felt that the new, younger employees were not making an effort to do accurate work. As the discussion continued, it became clear that there were certain typed reports in which no errors were acceptable. There were reports used within the department in which no one cared about errors.

When expectations are clear. . . performance improves

My next question for the supervisor, as you might guess, is "Do the new workers know and understand when they can and when they can't turn in reports with mistakes?" Typically, a supervisor's answer is, "Well, they should know."

Me: "But, do they know?"
Supervisor: "To tell the truth, I'm really not sure."

When the employee clearly understands what is expected, his performance will improve. But any working supervisor knows that the task is often more complicated. New employees may not be able to perform up to the standard immediately. On some jobs, it takes a day or two to learn how to do the job. On others, it takes years. **The supervisor needs to decide and come to terms with the employee on a reasonable level of performance.** When we train new salespeople, initially, all we expect is that they will make calls. However, if they continue month after month to make their calls, but never close a sale, we would be very unhappy.

The reason we hire people is to do a specific job, and our goal is that their performance match the standard as quickly as possible. The more a supervisor knows about the tasks he/she supervises, the easier it is to help an employee progress toward satisfactory performance.

A common trap is to get caught up in the reasons a person doesn't perform before we decide specifically what the performance problem is. In the example given of the younger workers who turned in work with mistakes, if we began by talking about the younger generation, generation gaps and differences between values, we might totally overlook the possibility that the workers did not clearly understand the standards.

When there are problems in performance, it is a good idea to start by talking to the employees. Explain the problem to them. Try to be as specific as you can. Ask for their opinion about the problem and about possible solutions. As you discuss the problem with them, your goal should be to reach a clear understanding about the differences between what they are doing and what is expected.

Try to identify any problems related to the work that may make it difficult to perform as expected. If there are personal problems that the employee shares with you that are interfering with the performance, you should lend a sympathetic ear, but be careful not to get so caught up in the problem that you are willing to continually accept poor performance from the employee. **Most supervisors are willing to make some adjustments for an employee who has an occasional, temporary problem.** However, if the problem is chronic, such as a drinking or drug problem that interferes with work performance, or a person who has severe and continual family problems that interfere with performance, we need to make some decisions. Are there steps we can take to help relieve the problem or is it time to terminate an employee

who is unable to produce the expected performance?

The key question is "Specifically what do you want the employee to do that's different from what he is doing now?" It's important to be able to use examples as you talk with him about his performance. It's better to say, "the last report you typed had ten errors per page," than, "you're making too many errors lately." If possible, you should have a copy of the report for reference as you discuss the problem. Let them know what the standard is. You might say something like, "We try to send out reports that are completely free of errors. We realize that occasionally (once or twice a week), a report will go out with an error in it. Any more errors than that are unacceptable." It's important to set realistic standards. If you tell someone that absolutely no mistakes are acceptable, when you know that an occasional error slips through, you run the risk of losing your credibility. **There is also a danger of creating so much pressure that it will take employees three times as long to do a job because they are afraid of making an error.**

If you set high, but reachable goals for your employees, communicate them clearly, and are open to questions about those goals and discussions, you're on your way to motivating your employees. When you don't get the performance you want, be sure to talk first about performance, and then after you are clear about performance expectations, explore the reasons for the problem. Once you know the reasons for the problem, find a way to resolve the problem. Don't get trapped into accepting the reason for the problem as an excuse for continuing poor performance.

MOTIVATORS THAT WORK

Here are a dozen of the common motivators and some ideas about the usefulness of these motivators to supervisors. But first, a word of caution to the readers. Sometimes reading a book like this is a bit like listening to a weather forecast on the radio or television. The forecaster tells us "fair skies and pleasant temperatures." Now even though the forecaster's overall batting average is pretty good, most of us will still look out the window to see for ourselves whether or not we need a raincoat.

We can tell you which motivators generally work, in fact, you'll find our predictions, overall, to be very accurate. However, in the same way that you decide for yourself whether or not to wear a raincoat or to take your umbrella, you ultimately have to make your own decisions about which motivators will work for you, in your work setting.

To decide whether your motivators are motivating, ask yourself two very important questions. The first question is, **"Are my employees doing what I want them to do, in the quality and quantity that's expected?"** If the answer is "no," then your motivators aren't motivating. If the answer is "yes," then you're on the right track, but you have to ask, and answer, the second question— **"Are there any undesirable side effects when I use a particular motivator?"** Let's take a look at some examples.

1.

MONEY Yes! Most employees will tell you that money is one of the most important reasons for working. However, from a supervisor's point of view, money is not the best motivator because supervisor's don't have enough control over the amount of money an employee gets. Even from a manager's point of view, money has limited potential as a motivator because if he pays too much, he doesn't make a profit. It's foolish to say that money is not a motivator, but the wise supervisor recognizes that it's only part of motivation, and that on a day-by-day basis other non-tangible factors are more important.

2.

PRAISE Praise is one of the most powerful motivators supervisors can use. Using praise as a motivator is an art. Praise needs to be genuine. The person praising the work should understand the work and recognize quality performance. Praise needs to be well timed. If work is only praised at set times, such as at the end of the work week or in a regularly-scheduled meeting, it tends to lose some of its impact. Good work should be recognized as it happens. People need to know that you appreciate their efforts.

3. **FEAR** Fear definitely does motivate people. But fear is not a a particularly good motivator for a supervisor to use. When we talk about fear as a motivator, we generally mean fear of losing something. Very often the fear of losing one's job, which is a natural consequence for poor performance, is a motivator. People will try to do what's expected in order to keep their jobs. **The problem is that when people work only because they are afraid, they tend to be very cautious and will seldom take any risks, seldom perform beyond what is dictated.**

When using fear as a motivator means threatening someone's self-esteem by embarrassing them with a severe reprimand, particularly in front of other people, we will sometimes get the performance we want, but often get other kinds of side effects that we really don't want. **When we consistently use fear as a motivator, employees become resentful and are more likely to slow down on the job, steal from the company, bad-mouth management, or join a union.**

Fear is also most effective in dealing with people who have very few options. When people feel trapped in a job situation, they will put up with less-desirable conditions. Very few American workers are so trapped that they will respond to fear as a motivator for any length of time. Also remember that if fear is a main theme in a work setting there will be a continued feeling of resentment. A clear understanding of natural consequences is a better motivator than fear. When people know what's expected and feel that they can perform up to expectations, and when they understand that continued performance is necessary to keep the position, you will get the desired results.

4. **CHALLENGE** Challenge is another of the motivators that a skillful supervisor can use to get high performance from employees. Once employees have the basic skills necessary for performance on their job and are comfortable at that basic level, they can also be motivated to do more work by presenting them with problems and tasks that are more difficult. **People enjoy a challenge when they also feel that they have the basic know-how and skills to solve the problem or complete the task.** In order for challenge to be an effective motivator, people need to feel comfortable in doing things on their own and occasionally making a mistake. If there is only one way to do the job—if mistakes are severely punished, then challenge will not work as a motivator. Skilled supervisors often turn routine assignments into challenges by assigning work in a way that gives a person a little bit more responsibility, by presenting a task in a way that points out the opportunity for an employee to perform at a new level and by encouraging him to see what he can do with a particular assignment. In fact, when you watch a skillful supervisor in action, you will find that the motivation has more to do with the way the work is presented than the actual work that is assigned.

5. **RESPONSIBILITY** Responsibility is another of the very powerful tools that a supervisor has to work with. **When employees assume ownership of the work assignments and the problems encountered, they are more likely to complete the work on time and perform at the expected levels.** For a supervisor to use responsibility as a motivator, that supervisor has to learn to turn loose of projects, give employees some choices as to how they get the work done, and must also assume that the employee has the basic ability to do the job. Sometimes when we ask employees to be responsible, we sabotage that effort by checking up too often, and making decisions for the employees as they encounter problems.

Clear goal setting at the beginning of a task or assignment is essential. Supervisors need to agree with the employee on the essential parts of the assignment and the deadlines as he begins the task. It should be clear at the beginning which decisions the employee can make on his own. If there are no decisions employees can make as they perform the task, and they simply do as they are told, then we would say they are "obedient" rather than responsible.

6. **RECOGNITION Recognition means that we let employees know that we are aware that they are doing their job, and we appreciate it.** Sometimes recognition takes note of outstanding performance as in "Employee of the Month" program, and awards, and bonuses for meeting and exceeding goals. Where supervisors often miss their chance is in recognizing employees who regularly perform at an ordinary level. If you watch effective supervisors, you'll find them taking a moment now and them to tell an employee that they appreciate the fact they can depend on the employee to be there on time every day. Sometimes, dependability is a greater asset than outstanding performance, particularly if you can't count on the outstanding performance.

7. **PROMOTIONS** Promotions are a good motivator when the individual you are trying to motivate wants a promotion, thinks that it is possible to be promoted, and would like the added responsibility that usually comes with promotion. **Supervisors who have been promoted and enjoyed added responsibility tend to think that everyone else wants a promotion.** The fact is that many of our employees do not particularly want to be promoted, and that even those who do want to be promoted recognize that there are relatively few chances for promotions in most organizations.

8.

INVOLVEMENT Involvement is one of the major ways that supervisors motivate employees. They let them know what's going on. They explain how the tasks that are assigned fit into the overall picture, and they ask for input from the employee. They do the things that make the employee feel that his contributions are important. When employees' contributions are important, employees feel better about themselves, and we know that people with a good self-image are likely to perform better work.

9.

LOYALTY Loyalty is a two-way process. We hope that the employee will feel loyal to the organization for that reason, work enthusiastically, share his ideas about improving production or services, and generally be pleasant to work with. However, to get that kind of loyalty from an employee, supervisors also have to be loyal to the employee. Loyalty exists when there is trust between supervisor and employee. and when the employee feels that the supervisor is fair and predictable. For this sense of loyalty to exist, employees also need to know that supervisors will back them up when there is a problem, will present their views to management, and will generally act in a way that recognizes the needs of the employees. **Loyalty is not something you can automatically expect from an employee.** It's something that grows over a period of time, and an issue in which new employees will take their cues from employees already on the job. Once that sense of loyalty is established, it is probably one of the strongest of the motivators supervisors can use.

10.

FRINGE BENEFITS Good fringe benefits, insurance, retirement programs, good equipment to work with, and pleasant offices help keep an organization going and improve the overall atmosphere. However, on a day-to-day basis, they are not nearly as powerful in motivating employees as the non-tangibles such as praise, and involvement, and loyalty. **Good fringe benefits keep people coming back to work and reduce turnover, and are an important part of an overall motivation program, but by themselves, will not get the enthusiastic, cooperative response that we look for when we talk about motivated employees.**

11.

REPRIMANDS A skillfully executed reprimand can be a very powerful motivator. Consistent, daily reprimands demoralize employees. But, a well-timed discussion about unsatisfactory performance can be very effective. A skillful reprimand is related to specific job goals, is done immediately after the unsatisfactory performance, and takes about one minute. You need to let the person know why his performance was unsatisfactory, let them know how you feel about it, and at the same time, remind the employee that you continue to value him for his continued good performance in other areas. Don't repeat the reprimand; don't smile while you do it; start with the things you are unhappy about, finish with the assurance that you still value the person and his overall performance.

12.

WORK Believe it or not, most people like to work. They may grumble and groan but they still derive pleasure and satisfaction from performing a task, particularly one they are comfortable doing. They enjoy developing their skills and are proud of their accomplishments. Supervisors sometimes forget how important the work itself can be. The more you can do as a supervisor to help workers develop skills, the better workers will feel about their jobs. Very often the best motivator or reward for doing a good job is to assign more work, work related to employee skills and interest. Remember that in our culture we often define our worth as human beings by the work we are able to do. We want to feel useful, needed and productive. Once basic needs, wages, health care, etc. are met, the work itself becomes a very important motivator.

As a supervisor it's important to tell workers that what they are doing is important. Ask them what parts of the job they like to do. Watch to see what they do best and whenever possible match interests, and work assignments.

Keep people busy. If you're having problems between workers, put them to work. Generally there are fewer problems when people are busy and productive.

As you try to decide which motivators are going to be most effective in your setting, remember that it's important to match the motivator to your own situation and to the people you work with. **Different strokes for different folks!**

16

TRUST

Honesty is the best policy. If you want your employees to trust you, if you want them to feel a sense of loyalty to you and the organization, you have to be fair, honest and consistent. Now, I know that sounds like something straight out of the Girl Scout manual; like something you would recite with one hand over your heart, and the other hand raised in the air with a victory signal. **Yet, honesty is a prerequisite to getting cooperation from employees.**

It's fun to talk to groups of supervisors about fair, honest and consistent. When I ask them, "Do you think it's important to be honest?" initially everyone says, "Yes, it is important to be honest." But, if you wait long enough and have created an atmosphere that's comfortable, one of those supervisors will tell about the problems of being honest. They say it's hard to be honest when people really don't want to hear the truth anyway. They will tell you that it's impossible to treat employees alike, and so you can't be fair, and that it's even difficult to be consistent, especially if you did something really dumb yesterday, and now feel like you should repeat the mistake again for the sake of consistency.

It would be naive to tell someone in the working world that you must always tell an employee exactly what's going on. Because the fact of the matter is that a supervisor has a great deal of privileged information — such as information regarding personnel that is the business only of the supervisor and the person concerned. Often, production plans, particularly in highly competitive businesses, are not to be shared. Very often, plans for layoffs, or expansions, or new products cannot be shared. **A good working guideline is to either tell them the truth or tell them that you can't share the information.**

It's impossible to treat everyone alike. And furthermore, it really isn't necessary. Supervisors have to make a lot of decisions about how to handle specific employee situations. To be fair, the supervisor should first fix clearly in his or her mind what the performance standard is. What is this person's job, and how is the current decision or problem related to his job performance? Next, **you need to know what the rules are, and how closely are they followed.** For example, there are usually fairly firm rules about how many days of work one can miss, how many personal or vacation days can be taken. But generally, a supervisor has some input into deciding whether a particular day off is a vacation day, a sick day or a personal day. Supervisors make informal decisions every day whether someone should be called into an office for a reprimand, or whether a particular problem should be documented and steps for termination begun.

It's impossible to treat everyone alike.

Most supervisors initially give an employee the benefit of the doubt, and usually that's a good practice. **It's a mistake, however, to accept poor performance from any employee on a continuing basis.**

It's a good idea to try very hard to be consistent in your dealings with employees. If employees know what to expect from you, they will trust you. They may disagree violently with what you do, but if they know that they are going to get the same kind of treatment every time, they will be more likely to trust you than if they can't predict what is going to happen.

If you want to handicap someone, withhold information, particularly information needed to perform a job. Don't let them know exactly why they are doing a job. Don't let them communicate with anyone else who is doing another part of the job. None of us would do that intentionally because it's pretty obvious that we don't get the kind of performance we want under those conditions. But in reality, many workers perform under handicaps like those because we haven't worked hard enough to be sure everyone knows what's going on.

If you attempt to be honest and consistent with

your employees, they will probably feel that you are fair. Your goal as a supervisor is to gain their trust and respect. **Once employees know that you are fair and are concerned about their needs, they will give you their loyalty.** When employees are loyal to a supervisor, many other things become much easier. They will overlook your "grouchy moods," and in fact, will cover for you when you make a mistake.

Motivation relies heavily on a cooperative atmosphere. Without a spirit of cooperation, the best instructions in the world, the highest wages and the best working conditions won't get you the kind of continuing performance that you need to run a successful organization. **Without trust, supervision becomes a continual game, and an adversary game at that.**

Self Motivation

A supervisor deals with employees on a day-by-day face-to-face basis. **When you're right there eyeball-to-eyeball, it's pretty hard to fake motivation.** In fact, at times, the whole process of getting ourselves motivated seems totally impossible. Fortunately, there are some fairly simple steps that we can take to get ourselves going.

Let's take a look at one of these self-motivated creatures to see if we can get a hint or two about how to motivate ourselves. To begin with, they always seem to know what they are doing and what they are going to do next. They also have a sense of urgency about them. They act like what they are doing is important and it's fairly hard to distract them from their task. Because they know where they are going and, seem to know how their jobs fit into the overall scheme of things, they are able to make most of the decisions about their work themselves. Self-motivators also know what they are doing and have the skills necessary to do their work. In reality, they probably aren't any smarter than anyone else but they take the time to practice or improve their skills when necessary to acomplish their goals. And, finally, the thing that's very pleasant about working with self-motivated people is that they're generally in a good mood. You'd be in a good mood, too, if there weren't so many frustrations and problems in your work. **What these self-motivated creatures have learned is that careful planning eliminates many of the frustrations and converts some of the other problems from major roadblocks to steps to climb on the way toward a goal.**

The easiest person to motivate and change is yourself. You understand yourself better than anyone else does, you know what you like to do and what you don't like to do. Start by doing a short self-inventory. The first question is **"Would you hire yourself to do your job?"** Do you know anyone who could do the job better than you're doing it now? What's the difference between that person, who would be better at your job, and yourself? What would you have to do to upgrade your performance.

Whenever we talk about motivation, the first question we have to ask is: "Motivated?....to do what?" "What are the priorities in your job?" "What are they paying you to accomplish through the people you supervise?" One of the first steps in tuning up your performance as a supervisor is to clarify your responsibilities. Make an appointment with your manager and go over the priorities. Before you go in, work them out as well as you can for yourself. List the major projects that you are working on currently and decide what you think the priorities are for these tasks. Then go over the tasks and the deadlines with your boss. Try to set goals on a monthly or quarterly basis for your department.

Then after the conference, take time to plan the steps toward those goals. **Decide what to do first and who should do it.** Anything that one of your employees can possibly do for you should be delegated to that person. When you think about delegating, take a moment to decide how the work fits into the overall responsibilities of that employee, how long you think it will take him to accomplish this and what kind of assistance he will need to complete the job. The moment or two you take now will prepare you to discuss the assignment with the employee. Work out a plan for, at least, the next month. Then decide what part of that plan you can accomplish during the next week and break that part into a day-by-day schedule.

Effective planning requires paper and pencil. You absolutely have to write down your goals. List both long-range and short-term goals.

The trouble that most folks have with planning is that, once they get into the heat of the battle, they forget what the plan was or, at least, get distracted for periods of time.

One of the most helpful tricks I know to keep yourself on the track is to write down your goals for the day and for the week and put it where you can see it while you work. If you have a goal that you're working on that requires a change in your own behavior, like losing or gaining weight or being more friendly to people, write a note and put it on the bathroom mirror, or cover it in saran wrap and put it in the shower. Put a note in your car. Write your goal for the day on your calendar.

So, you can see that the steps toward becoming a self-motivated supervisor are really very simple. First of all, be crystal clear that what you're trying to accomplish fits the goals of the organization. They are paying you for performance and **you need to be sure that you are performing the right tasks.**

During the times in your life when you're trying to upgrade your job performance, or just accomplish a little more of the important things in your life, it helps to have a model.

Would you hire yourself to do your job?

Pick someone who gets lots of things accomplished, who shares your values and who does it all in a style that makes some sense to you. Watch how they work. Talk to them. Find out what kind of planning they do. It's particularly helpful if you have a model you know fairly well. If you try to model yourself after someone you read about in a magazine, all you know is the good stuff. **In real life, the people who are accomplishing lots of things, performing very well on their job and generally having a good time, aren't much different than you or I.** And when we find a real live person who eats and sleeps and sweats just like we do, then it's easier for us to realize we could be accomplishing the same things.

I used to think self-discipline was a dirty word. I thought it was important to be spontaneous, to be in touch with your feelings and to make the most of the moment. What I've discovered since then, and learned from lots of supervisors, is that **without self-discipline, you accomplish little or nothing.** The fact of the matter is that if you discipline yourself and do the unpleasant things as well as the pleasant, you have more time and, often, more money to do what you really want to do. Self-discipline is an essential part of self-motivation.

Self-discipline means creating routines for yourself that work. It means getting control of crises and interruptions on your job. It may mean putting a clock where you can see it to reduce the amount of time you spend on the phone. **Self-discipline means resisting the temptation to give up on a priority task before it is finished.** Self-discipline means reminding yourself that this is a priority task and paying more attention, at times, to long-range goals than to immediate pleasure. Self-discipline also means learning to say "no." Some of us have grown up placing such a value on relationships and acceptance by other people that it is very difficult to resist trying to do everything for everybody.

Self Motivation

A problem some of us have in motivating ourselves is overcoming a negative self-image. If you spent years seeing yourself as a follower rather than a leader, it may require a bit of effort to get things turned around. You may not realize how much input you're getting from T.V. and magazine advertising that tells you that you should be something you're probably not ever going to be.

Women, particularly, have an almost impossible task of measuring up to the models of T.V. and magazine advertising. Unless you're 18 years old, weigh 100 pounds, are 5 feet, 11 inches and have a perfect complexion, you don't meet the standard. And, even if you do, you're soon going to be 19. For men, the range is a little wider; even Burt Reynolds wears a toupee. To have a realistic and positive self-image, you need to decide for yourself what's important and focus on things that you can do something about. If you're 6 feet, 10 inches, and unhappy about it, there's not much you can do, short of amputating your feet. On the other hand, if you're unhappy about continually being late for work, it's a fairly simple matter to make a decision to change. Set an alarm clock or two and get up and go to work twenty minutes earlier.

A nice technique for reminding yourself what a good guy or gal you really are, is to take a moment and list on a piece of paper at least ten things that you do well on your job. Think about your work habits. Do you get to work on time? Do you have a good attendance record? Do you manage your time well? What job skills do you have? Can you type? Are you a good welder? Do you have mechanical ability? Are you good at working with people? How do you handle yourself in a crisis? That's only the beginning. Pick out the things you do well and write them down. Imagine that you're about to sell yourself to another employer. Most of us spend far too much time thinking about the things we do poorly and telling ourselves what bad people we are and too little time focusing on the things we do well. **When we pay more attention to the things we do well, we seem to have more energy to work on the things that still need improvement.**

Now that you've made a big long list of things you do well, make a shorter list, three to five items, of the things you would like to do a bit differently in your work. Should you dress a little bit differently on this job? Do you need to follow-up on the work of your employees more effectively? Should you do something different to meet or beat a deadline that is coming up? Do you need to eliminate some things that you do at work that waste time, such as personal phone calls, allowing yourself to be interrupted or not finishing one job before you start another?

Once you make up your mind that you are going to get yourself going, and you have clear goals that match those of your employer, and a clear idea where to begin, you're on your way. **To stay on the track, be sure that your goals are written and pay attention to your accomplishments.** When you run into a problem or a snag, define the problem as a challenge rather than a failure. Realize that you are going to make some mistakes and do some really dumb things. Use a mistake as a learning opportunity and try not to make the same mistake over again. Once you get into the routine of deciding for yourself what you are going to do, and following through with those plans, you'll never go back again to letting someone else make the decisions for you. **Success is a habit that's hard to break.**

WORK CLIMATE

The moment you walk into a store, a factory, a business, a school or a service organization, you begin to form an opinion about the place. Your opinion is based on details like: **Does anyone greet you? Is anyone smiling? Does anyone care that you just walked in the door? Is the place neat and tidy, or is it a total mess?**

One of my favorite businesses is a small garage run by a middle-aged man with a European accent. The garage is spotless, and everything is clean and in its place. On the desk in the small office next to his garage, all you see are an appointment book, receipts, phone and directory. The man is polite, but business-like. **Everything about the man and his establishment communicates craftmanship, competence and reliability.**

What are the messages that are conveyed by your work setting? How do employees feel about working for your organization? When we say "work climate," we're talking about how it feels to work in your organization. You can get some idea of how people feel about working in your organization by looking at our checklist of problems related to the work climate. Look the list over and check the items that you feel apply to your organization.

PROBLEM CHECKLIST

1. Employees Steal From the Company ____

2. Employees Steal From Each Other ____

3. Average Absenteeism Over Ten Days a Year Per Employee ____

4. Supervisors Don't Know All First Names of Their Employees ____

5. People Don't Acknowledge Each Other When They Pass in Aisles and Halls ____

6. Audible Sign of Relief When Boss Leaves ____

7. Employees Vandalize Company Restrooms, Lunch Rooms, Bulletin Boards ____

8. Deadlines are Overrun ____

9. Work Places Dirty, Disorganized ____

10. Employees Line Up At Time Clock Earlier Every Day at Quitting Time ____

MORE PROBLEMS

11. When in Doubt, Employees Stop Rather Than Risk Making a Mistake   _____

12. Supervisors and Managers Who Scream at Employees   _____

13. Bosses Who Overlap and Give Conflicting Instructions to Employees   _____

14. Excessive Turnover   _____

15. Sabotaged Products   _____

17. Work Stoppage When a Supervisor is Not Present   _____

18. Feeling That Promotions are Unfair   _____

19. Employees Supersensitive to Criticism   _____

20. Nagging Feeling on Your Part That Employees Aren't Doing Their Best Job   _____

21. Employees Work Two Jobs to Make a Living   _____

22. Employees Feel It Doesn't Matter What They Do as Long As They Put In Their Time   _____

23. Excessive Safety Violations   _____

24. If You Don't Understand This Memo, Wait. The Next One Will Be Different   _____

25. Workers Apologize When They Tell Their Friends Where They Work   _____

Go back and look over the items you checked. In your setting, are these items you checked serious problems? Are these conditions making it difficult for employees to feel like working? And, is there anything you can do about the problems that you checked?

Let's take a look at some of the factors that contribute to a productive, pleasant working environment. Again, check the ones you feel apply in your own situation.

TANGIBLES	
1. Good to adequate wages	_____
2. Profit-sharing plan	_____
3. Good vacation plan	_____
4. Safe working conditions	_____
5. Pleasant working environment	_____
6. Adequate to good retirement program	_____
7. Bonuses paid	_____
8. Compensation related to performance	_____
9. Special "goodies" provided	_____
• Company discounts	_____
• Health and recreation facilities	_____
• Work clothing provided	_____
• Conventions and conferences	_____

INTANGIBLES	
1. Praise and recognition for good work	_____
2. Employees' ideas solicited	_____
3. Challenge provided	_____
4. Information shared	_____
5. Employees proud of the company	_____
6. Employees loyal to the company	_____
7. Promotions possible	_____
8. Opportunities to learn and grow	_____
9. Pleasant colleagues	_____
10. Variety in work assignments	_____

As you look over the items that you've checked, see if there is a balance between the tangible and the intangible motivators. An effective organization tries to strike a balance. Organizations which are heavy on intangibles and short on tangibles tend to wear their people out. Typically this problem is found in places like social service agencies, public schools or small businesses. The work is interesting, employees are committed to what they do, but the wages are low and the benefits minimal.

On the other hand, there are some organizations, typically large corporations with thousands of employees, where wages and vacations are good, insurance is provided, and there may be a whole smorgasbord of special "goodies," but at the same time employees feel that they are just a number, and that no one really cares about them as people. Employees also wear out in this kind of organization. But when pay and benefits are so good, employees may feel that they can't afford to leave, so they simply retire on the job. The most productive organizations are those that strike a balance between the tangible and intangible benefits.

A good working climate should be comfortable, yet people should understand that they are being paid for what they produce, not simply existing in the place. Employees should feel that their contribution is important to the overall functioning of the organization. They should also get regular feedback about their performance and praise for what they do well.

In most organizations, supervisors can do little about the tangible rewards for work. It's true that they can sometimes fire a person and completely take away the tangible rewards, but by and large, upper management makes the decisions about wages, vacations and fringe benefits. On the other hand, no matter what management decides about the intangible rewards, these cannot be provided without the help of a supervisor. Some of the things that a supervisor can do in almost any organization that make a critical difference in the work climate are:

1. **Get to know your people.** Offer a friendly greeting at the beginning of each workday; talk to them occasionally about outside interests. Let them know that you care about them as individuals.

2. **Give clear assignments.** Get their input about the job; be sure employees have a chance to ask questions about the work that's being assigned.

3. **Follow-up.** After assigning work, be sure that it's being done correctly.

4. **Give plenty of feedback.** Let people know if their work is on or off the track. Expect new workers to make some mistakes. When the performance is off the track, assume first that the instructions were not clear, and clarify the expectations.

5. **Don't ignore non-performance.** As soon as you realize someone is not doing the job, check to see what's happening. Let the worker know that you expect performance.

6. **Praise workers who do what's expected of them.** A pay check is not sufficient for a job adequately done. It's easy to praise exceptional work, but you should be grateful and recognize employees who regularly perform their work adequately.

7. **Don't throw tantrums and scream at employees** without thinking about it for at least an hour. It doesn't hurt at all to let employees know what they've done has really upset you, but routinely screaming only irritates people and is not particularly effective. If you like to scream and throw tantrums, be sure you don't do it more than once a month.

Finally, remember that the most important intangible part of the work climate is a healthy sense of self-esteem. When workers feel good about themselves, about the company and the work they do, it will be much easier to get cooperation from them.

LISTENING

To motivate employees, you need to know something about them. Most of us are aware that the same things don't motivate all employees. It's important to get to know them as individuals. It helps if you know what things interest your employees, what kind of work they like to do best, what, if anything they want to learn in addition to their current job responsibilities, and it also helps to know a little about their families and personal lives. It helps to know what kind of hobbies and outside interests they have. Are they on a bowling team? Do they race ponies and dragsters or bicycles? Do they like to fish or hunt? Or, do they just like to sit home and drink beer and watch TV?

You also want to know what kind of problems employees are having on the job. It helps to know what kind of assignments they like and dislike. You can also benefit from any ideas they have about how to do the job they work at every day.

Some people are simply easier to talk to than others. Let me tell you the story about my gruff old farmer grandfather. Grandfather was the head of the family of nine boys and six girls, obviously in the days before "zero population" growth. My mother and aunts and uncles delight in telling a story about the time Grandpa decided to drive into town in his Model T. In this family, a trip to town was a special occasion, and before he left, at least half of the family had piled into his car. As the story is retold, no one is quite sure about how many started out in the car. Probably no one knew on that day either. As they set out for town, Grandpa had gotten a little more than irritated at his noisy passengers and threatened to put anyone who made another sound out of the car. The kids knew that he meant business, and knew better than to irritate him any further, so they stopped hollering and yelling, and entertained each other by making faces, punching and pinching, and taking turns leaning out the back window as far as they could. Aunt Mary won the leaning contest — she leaned out so far that she fell out and tumbled into the ditch. The remaining passengers were terrified — terrified that Mary "broke her neck," but even more terrified about what Grandpa would say when he found out. It wasn't until five miles later that anyone had the courage to tell him what had happened.

Some work situations are a little like my Grandpa and his car full of kids. Even when a worker really should ask questions, or tell someone about a problem, it seems easier to keep quiet.

It's important for a supervisor to do whatever he or she can to create an atmosphere where people are comfortable in sharing ideas and asking questions. Here are some suggestions that you can use to get the input you need to run an effective department.

MOTIVATES

1. **BE AVAILABLE.** Remember that it is possible to say you are available, but still be unapproachable. If no one comes to you, if they don't ask, maybe they are afraid or put off by your manner.

2. **LET PEOPLE KNOW THAT YOU HAVE THE TIME TO TALK WITH THEM AND TO ANSWER THEIR QUESTIONS.** You can create this open atmosphere for communication if you take the initiative and spend a moment or two each day with your employees. Stop by and say "hello." Ask how their job is going. Give them a chance to talk about problems.

3. **TAKE QUESTIONS AND SUGGESTIONS SERIOUSLY.** If you really do take the time to listen to employees, some of them are going to ask questions and make suggestions that from your point of view, seem to be pretty dumb or naive. Hear them out, particularly when their comments seem to be coming from left field and don't make any sense at all. Make an effort to understand their point of view, and give them a chance to explain. If you simply wait a moment or two before responding, you will give them the message that you are taking them seriously.

4. **LEARN TO BE A GOOD LISTENER.** When someone comes to you with a problem, whether it's related to job or to their personal life, take the time to listen to them, ask questions about the problem, find out what possible solutions they have considered, try to determine how they feel about the problem. Is it serious or only a minor irritation? Withhold any advice until you have listened to them for at least three minutes. Even when someone comes to you and asks for advice, it's a good idea to explore the problem and try to find out what they have already attempted as solutions before you offer your gems of wisdom.

5. If you want employees to be comfortable in coming to you, you must be careful not to repeat any confidential or sensitive information they share with you.

The benefits of listening and getting as much input as possible from your employees are:

- A feeling of trust between employees and supervisors

- A greater sense of loyalty on the part of employees

- Lots of information from employees about work progress and problems

- Help from employees in solving problems

- A generally pleasant work atmosphere

- More work accomplished

Reprimands

As we talk about motivation, it's easy to get so involved in ways of creating a positive work climate, that we sometimes forget to face the reality of how to deal with employees whose performance is unacceptable. Like it or not, part of the job of the supervisor is to reprimand employees. The problem is, "how do you get the message across that you're unhappy with what they are doing or not doing, and at the same time, help them maintain their sense of self-worth and dignity?" **Here is a simple format that will help you be extremely effective.**

1. **Don't smile.** The moment you smile, even though you are trying to put the person at ease, you have reduced your effectiveness. Smiling indicates approval, and you are talking about performance that does not have your approval.

2. **Don't gunny-sack.** Gunny-sacking is saving up all of your complaints and problems until the bag is full and then dumping it on the employee. Reprimand as soon as possible after the problem occurs.

3. **Be specific.** Tell the person what he or she did wrong. Tell them what you observed and how that differs from what is expected. Give them a chance to clarify the issue. But don't accept "excuses."

4. **Tell them how you feel** about what they did or did not do. If you are surprised, or angry or disappointed, tell them; and then pause long enough that they can share your unpleasant feeling.

5. **Put the reprimand into perspective.** Let them know how much you value them as an employee. Reaffirm that you think well of them, but not of their performance in this situation.

6. **Don't repeat the reprimand.** Realize that when the reprimand is over, you are finished.

The whole process described above need not take over three to five minutes.

Reprimand when. . .

1. An employee **does not perform** an assigned task, and. . .

2. There is no question that the **assignment was clear,** and. . .

3. The employee definitely made a **commitment to perform,** and. . .

4. The assignment was **realistic,** and. . .

5. The supervisor has the **respect** of the employee.

If any of the above is missing, the reprimand will not be effective.

Personal Power

To be a supervisor requires an understanding of personal power. You don't need to be able to make a speech about personal power or write a book about it, or even to be able to explain it to your neighbor. All you really need is an understanding of what works and the ability to give directions in a way that people are willing to follow. Some people seem to do it naturally, and couldn't explain what they are doing if their life depended on it. Others of us stumble about for a bit, and are not as sure or confident about how to proceed. **Anyone can learn to be a good leader.** If you are not naturally good at it, your first attempts may be clumsy and not so successful. To become a skillful leader requires practice and experience. It's unrealistic to expect instant success. But, it is possible to learn and one of the best ways to learn is to observe good leaders and model ourselves after them.

Employees expect to be given direction. They hope the directions will be clear; they hope they will be able to perform the work, and they expect the distribution of the work to be more or less fair.

The simple fact that you have the title of "supervisor," or have been assigned some supervision functions gives you a head start. This is the same sort of formal authority that a policeman has when he puts on a uniform, or that a doctor has when she hangs a stethoscope around her neck. In fact, the role of the supervisor is a little bit like the role of a traffic cop. If you come to an intersection and find a policeman standing in the middle of the street, particularly a policeman with a whistle or white gloves or a flashlight, you deduce from these not-so-subtle clues that he is there to direct traffic. You look to that person for direction.

Can you picture the situation in which, as you approach the intersection, you realize that the traffic cop is busy talking to someone on the curb. You know right away he isn't doing his job, he isn't directing traffic, and you don't pay much more attention to him. Or, perhaps there he stands in the middle of the intersection waving in 20 different directions at the same time, and as you approach him, he is screaming and yelling at you. Now, what happens? You get confused, angry, and you have to put a whole lot more effort into not getting arrested and not causing an accident. With someone like that directing traffic, you'd be better off at home.

Supervision is a little bit like directing traffic. **If you make the right moves and act like you know what you are doing, people are willing to follow your direction.** If you send out conflicting signals, workers don't know what's expected, and they get confused and upset.

Anyone can learn to be a good leader

So, the object is to capitalize on those first two things in your favor: 1. You are defined as the supervisor, and 2. People are expecting you to give leadership.

To be a good leader, you really should know what you are doing. You should know the job that you supervise, and the more you know about the job, the easier it will be to supervise. **But, it's unrealistic and unnecessary to try to know more about the job than any of the employees.** Even when you do know more about the job, it's still a good idea to ask how they think the job should be done, and to get their input about solving problems that arise. Asking for input keeps workers involved, and gives them a sense of responsibility for the task.

If you don't already know as much as you would like to about the job, make every attempt to upgrade your knowledge by observing what's going on, asking questions and occasionally performing a part of the job yourself. Be careful if you do perform a part of someone else's job, that they do not view your "stepping in" as an intrusion.

To exercise power as a supervisor demands more skill and finesse than is required of a manager. A manager at the top will always win in a showdown. A supervisor in a direct confrontation with an employee, particularly a union employee, may or may not win. Poor power users are always in the middle of a showdown, but the effective power people avoid confrontations. They manage to get the job done without a showdown.

To use power effectively requires some planning. **You don't go straight for the strangle-hold because that promotes resistance and survival tactics on the part of the stranglee.** Watch a good salesman in action. He starts by finding a common ground, where he can agree with the prospective customer. He sweetens his customer up ahead of time. If it's an Irish salesman, we call it "blarney." When the salesman is really good, the approach is friendly; there is genuine agreement about something. "It really is a nice day!" "That really is an attractive daughter standing there beside you." Even when you know what he's doing, you find yourself nodding your head in agreement.

If you work gently toward the issue that really does matter and ask the employee's opinion, ask what solutions he would consider, sometimes you'll find that he will come up with a good solution of his own. After all, he wants to get along, and doesn't want the confrontation either. So, if you make it possible for him to agree with you, save face, and maintain his dignity, very often he will come up with the very solution you had in mind, but offer it as his own. That's a very pleasant resolution to a difficult situation.

The supervisor who is effective in the use of power gains control in small steps. During the first days on the job, little is changed. She asks people to do what they have been doing all along, to do what they are used to doing. Even if it is clear from the beginning that things need to be changed, she establishes her power by giving orders that are easy to follow. **Then, once the pattern of following orders is established, she introduces the changes she wishes to make.**

Whenever you feel that you are about to be confronted on an issue, or that someone is going to resist you in public, find a way to deal with that person individually.

Supervisors who use power effectively have learned to speak clearly. Effective power users

say, "let's begin by doing 1-2-3." Ineffective power users say, "Don't you think we should be doing 1-2-3?"

There's a very important body language that goes along with power. Watch the people in your organization who are successful in giving orders and in leading people. You will probably find that they stand tall with their chin up, they look you straight in the eye, their eyes are steady, and they don't smile when giving directions.

The supervisor who uses power effectively also has an office or desk or working space that is well organized and uncluttered. There are no distractions; there is nothing to indicate that anything other than what is being discussed at the moment is important. If it looks as if he spent some time planning how the space looks and what effect it will have on subordinates, you're probably right!

Good supervisors also pay attention to the way they are dressed. As you look around your own organization, you can see the differences in dress and hair styles as people move up the organizational ladder. Sometimes the differences are subtle, and there are, of course, exceptions. If you are a new supervisor, it's a mistake to continue to dress more like your employees than like the other supervisors. The message you are sending out is that you have not totally taken over the role of supervisor.

As a supervisor, a good part of your power comes from upper management. So, it makes good sense to continually communicate with your own manager, letting him or her know what's going on in your department, and continually clarifying goals. **Nothing will sabotage your own personal power quicker than going off on a tangent and asking your employees to work in a way that is contrary to current management priorities.**

Finally, remember that even good and powerful supervisors make mistakes. Your credibility will suffer if you pretend that you haven't made a mistake when it is obvious to everyone else that you have. When you make a mistake, try to analyze what happened, pick up the pieces, get things back on the right track, and take steps to avoid making the same mistakes again.

Quality Circles

"Made in Japan" used to be a joke. If it was made in Japan, we expected it to be made out of old beer cans and to fall apart the first time we tried to use it. Made in Japan is no joke now. We all know that Japanese production and quality are such that they have become a serious threat to American businesses.

There is no one secret to the Japanese industrial recovery and success. The excellent quality and production that they are able to achieve are related to an intense and successful effort on the part of their government to restructure the whole fabric of Japanese society. They have carefully planned and developed their educational system, housing, transportation and their work methods more successfully than any other industrial nation.

One of the tools that seems to have application in American industry is the quality circle. In a quality circle, a group of workers (usually about ten) meet for an hour or so three or four times a month. **They talk about quality and production problems, and ways to solve other general problems in their area.** A foreman or possibly one of the workers may lead the group. If during the meeting they decide they don't have enough information to solve the particular problem, one or more of the workers may be assigned to collect information before they meet again. They implement whatever solutions they can on their own and also make recommendations to management about changes that require upper-level approval.

The results are astounding. **When the workers get involved in solving the problems, they sometimes resolve problems that have baffled the engineers and managers.** When quality circles work, profits increase, morale improves, absenteeism is reduced, and safety problems are quickly resolved.

The first United States firm to adopt the full quality circle concept was Lockheed Missile and Space Company in Sunnyvale, California. A group from Lockheed had visited Japanese companies and were amazed at what they found. They were impressed at how effective quality control circles motivated people by enriching their job and increasing their sense of participation. They were also impressed at the strong support top management gave to the program and the obvious commitment to making the quality circles work.

Lockheed introduced quality circles in their own company in October of 1974. By 1977, the company estimated that the circles had saved them three million dollars. The number of defects in the manufacturing process had declined by two-thirds, and they also found greatly improved morale and job satisfaction.

Made in Japan is no joke now

Some of the problems that workers resolved in the groups were as follows: one quality circle in a molding shop developed a way to make a plastic part in two steps instead of five. The new assembly was more reliable, wider and stronger, and produced savings of $160,000 over the life of a government contract. Another group of electronics assemblers saved $19,000 on a project by recommending a solution that improved the quality of a circuit board. Electronic components at Lockheed were identified by stamping on an identification number. In the past, the stamping ink faded on the shelf and parts often had to be restamped. A quality circle group developed a new ink with a longer shelf-life and saved the company $120,000 per year.

Quality circles have not been totally successful in the United States. Generally the problems encountered are related to existence of employees' unions or middle management. Sometimes the problem is that management itself is not totally committed to the idea. It needs to be clear to everyone involved that there is a payoff to them in that quality circles do not constitute a threat to their position or to their power. Workers who feel that quality circles benefit only management soon lose interest.

Supervisors should familiarize themselves with the concept of quality circles. Even if their company is not interested in establishing quality circles, there are some things to be learned from them.

Quality circles work because they are a way of applying the principles of motivation. In quality circles, we are asking for input from employees. We are providing as much information as possible about the company to keep them involved. We are listening to their ideas and communicating to the workers that their input is needed and their ideas are worthwhile. The most convincing part of the communication for the worker is seeing their own ideas actually implemented.

Supervisors who have staff meetings of any kind can implement some of the things from quality circles that work. **In meetings, give your people time to ask questions and present ideas they have.** To be successful at this, you need to learn to ask open-ended questions; such as, "What can we do to solve this problem?" And then, if you don't get immediate response, gently poll the group by asking the people involved in the problem what they have been thinking about the problem and what they would like to do to resolve the problem. To be successful in conducting this kind of group discussion, you need to learn to listen carefully to what people say, even if initially it seems like a ridiculous idea. As soon as you make fun of what people say, or tell them immediately that their idea won't work, or that it is naive, you will teach them to keep their ideas to themselves. It's also very important to try very hard to implement ideas that employees present. If they come up with solutions to problems that you can't implement on your own, that require upper-level management decisions, you also need to learn to communicate these ideas clearly to upper-level management. If possible, it's a good idea to include an employee in that presentation, and it's **always** important to give the employee credit for the idea. The first time you take the credit for one of their ideas will be the last time they share an idea with you.

One of the other things that make Japanese industries work so well is that the employees have an intense sense of loyalty to the company and to the work group. American society and business has a very different structure and feeling than the Japanese society, and it would be very difficult to duplicate that feeling. However, you can get workers more involved by doing some things to establish a group or department identity. Do what you can to look out for the needs of your department and let your people know what you are doing. When your group has a good production day or meets production goals, put a notice up — something that says "We Did It!" or "We Did It Again!" If you have a company newsletter or bulletin, be sure to take advantage of any opportunity to get a group picture in the bulletin. The people who write those newsletters for your company usually are looking for ideas and will welcome your suggestions. Some supervisors develop a sense of group identity and team work by buying the **group coffee when they have done well.** It seems ridiculous that the whole group would work for a 40¢ or 50¢ cup of coffee, but somehow or other the coffee is sweeter when the supervisor pays for it. And, what's really going on is that the supervisor is giving recognition to the group.

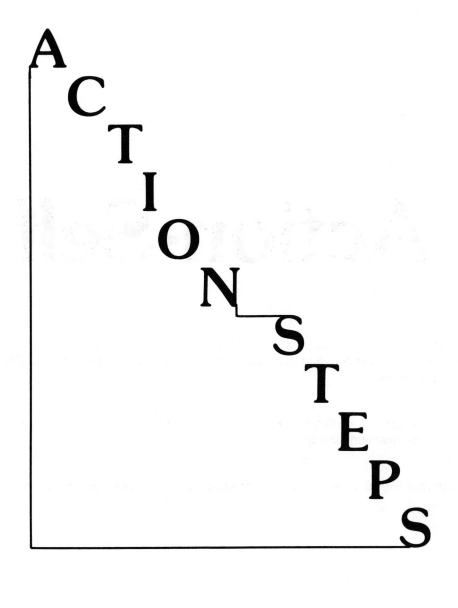

Action-Self

Now that you've thought about, and read about, motivation, what are you going to do to become even more effective at motivating employees? Remember, it's ACTION that will make the difference.

Here are a series of checklists to help you decide what to do next, to help you get your own motivation program underway.

We've started with Self-Motivation. Remember, your actions speak louder than words.

Checklist   # Self Motivation

	Good Shape Now	Action Needed
1. I know how to use personal power.	____	____
2. I plan my work regularly.	____	____
3. My job description is up-to-date.	____	____
4. I discuss priorities with my boss.	____	____
5. I plan job assignments ahead.	____	____
6. I would follow a leader like me.	____	____
7. I look like a supervisor.	____	____
8. I take care of my health.	____	____
9. I'm at a healthy weight.	____	____
10. I exercise regularly.	____	____
11. I like my job.	____	____
12. I'm an interesting person.	____	____
13. My job skills are up-to-date.	____	____
14. I have job goals for the next year.	____	____
15. I pay attention to success.	____	____
16. I learn from mistakes.	____	____
17. I feel like a part of management.	____	____
18. I'm a good model for employees.	____	____
19. I seek feedback from my boss.	____	____
20. I volunteer for interesting projects.	____	____

RELATIONSHIPS

Here's a checklist with a dozen ideas about actions that help supervisors develop positive working relationships with employees. Motivating employees means that you influence the way they perform their jobs. You have to have the relationships if you expect to gain cooperation and improve performance.

Look over the list and find the areas in which you need to take action.

TRUST — RELATIONSHIPS

	Good Shape Now	Action Needed
1. I know the first names of my employees.	____	____
2. I say hello to everyone every day.	____	____
3. I am able to smile in the morning.	____	____
4. I know at least one outside interest of each employee.	____	____
5. I can listen without giving advice.	____	____
6. My employees come to me with problems.	____	____
7. I'm good at getting input from employees.	____	____
8. I keep calm when things go wrong.	____	____
9. When I correct employees, they are willing to change what they are doing.	____	____
10. I give praise to someone each day.	____	____
11. I support my work group.	____	____
12. My employees would say I am "fair."	____	____

Ask for Performance

When you ask for performance, your workers will know what's expected and understand that you really do expect them to do quality work, and, at the same time, to meet the deadlines.

We know from experience that you can get performance. The odds are on the supervisor's side. You have to know what you want, give clear instruction, convey positive expectations, and make it easy for the worker to cooperate.

Look over the list — evaluate your own performance.

40

ASK FOR PERFORMANCE

	Good Shape Now	Action Needed
1. Each of my employees has a clear job description.	_____	_____
2. I give clear job assignments.	_____	_____
3. My workers meet their deadlines.	_____	_____
4. My group sometimes exceeds the minimum standards.	_____	_____
5. I monitor performance regularly.	_____	_____
6. I follow-up poor performance.	_____	_____
7. I have a written outline for training new employees.	_____	_____
8. I can reprimand effectively when necessary.	_____	_____
9. I'm successful at solving problems with employees.	_____	_____
10. I can leave for a day and expect output to hold up.	_____	_____
11. My employees are trained to do each other's jobs.	_____	_____
12. I reward good performers with praise and recognition.	_____	_____
13. I'm good at delegating.	_____	_____
14. I keep my workers informed and involved.	_____	_____
15. When problems arise, I focus on performance not personality.	_____	_____
16. I get agreement from employees on realistic deadlines.	_____	_____

The Setting

Finally, take a look at the setting. What's it like to work here? The way you keep house, the way you set up your offices and your plant, silently speaks to employees, telling them what is important, who is important, and where priorities really lie.

Score yourself on the setting. Think about the areas in which you could take action that would increase motivation.

THE SETTING

	Good Shape Now	Action Needed
1. My area is clean and orderly.	____	____
2. Bulletin boards are kept up-to-date.	____	____
3. Individual desks or work stations are kept clean and neat.	____	____
4. Supplies are available when needed.	____	____
5. Tools and machinery and equipment are well maintained.	____	____
6. Workers cooperate to keep the place clean and orderly.	____	____
7. Noise is controlled.	____	____
8. Workers have control over their own 'territory.'	____	____
9. Workers have input when areas are rearranged.	____	____
10. Our safety record is excellent.	____	____
11. Temperature is conducive to production.	____	____
12. Traffic patterns aid production.	____	____
13. Area is well illuminated.	____	____
14. Workers enjoy being here.	____	____

Action Plan

Here is a planning format to help you formulate a plan of Action.

Go back and look at the checklists. Identify the areas in which you feel ACTION is needed. Pick one to three areas and write them down here. Either write in the book or make a copy of the planning page.

EXAMPLE:

1. ACTION NEEDED

My job description needs to be updated.

3. SPECIFIC FIRST STEP

Make an appointment with manager.

3. ACTION DATE

Tomorrow A.M.

Put the planning sheet where you will see it and remember your good intentions.

Enjoy your success and remember that success is a tough habit to break!

ACTION PLAN

1.   ACTION NEEDED _____
_____
_____

     SPECIFIC FIRST STEP _____
_____
_____

     ACTION DATE _____

2.   ACTION NEEDED _____
_____
_____

     SPECIFIC FIRST STEP _____
_____
_____

     ACTION DATE _____

3.   ACTION NEEDED _____
_____
_____

     SPECIFIC FIRST STEP _____
_____
_____

     ACTION DATE _____

Reading List

There are many good books on motivation. The following are only a sampling of what can be found in most public libraries by anyone who is interested in learning more about *what* supervisors should do about motivation and *how* they can do it more effectively.

Most of the books on this list are still in print, some of them in relatively inexpensive paperback editions. If you want to add them to your personal library, look for them in your local bookstore or order them directly from the Products Department of Professional Training Associates, Inc., 212 Commerce Boulevard, Round Rock, TX 78664. Call 1-800-822-7824 for details.

Fournies, Ferdinand F. **Coaching for Improved Work Performance.** Fournies & Associates, 1978.

Shows that many "motivational" problems can be solved by using the coaching approach to improving performance. Demonstrates the coaching process with numerous case studies.

Halloran, Jack and George L. Frunzi. **Supervision: The Art of Management.** 2nd Edition. Prentice Hall, 1986.

Offers a systematic view of the supervisor's role and responsibilities, including employee motivation. Identifies and explains the skills and abilities that every supervisor needs to develop.

Losoncy, Lewis. **The Motivating Leader.** Prentice Hall, 1985.

Explains and illustrates more than 40 techniques for motivating people to *want* to do their best. Also offers realistic, positive solutions to such "people problems" as absenteeism, disrespect, irresponsibility, and stubbornness.

McLagan, Patricia and Peter Krembs. **On-the-Level: Performance Communication That Works.** McLagan International, 1988.

Focuses on the real-life communication problems that are often responsible for poor motivation, and outlines specific action steps for dealing with them. Takes the mystery out of "getting through to employees."

Quick, Thomas L. **Quick Solutions: 500 People Problems Managers Face & How to Solve Them.** John Wiley & Sons, 1987.

Describes—and resolves—most of the "sticky" situations that supervisors will ever face. Written in question-and-answer form with a detailed index that refers you right to the answer you need.

Sherman, V. Clayton. **From Losers to Winners: How to Manage Problem Employees—and What to Do If You Can't.** AMACOM, 1987.

Offers a clear, no-nonsense approach to dealing with problem employees. Covers all the "motivational" problems these employees represent. Explains how to handle problem behavior, apply stricter discipline when appropriate, and fire when necessary.

Sussman, Lyle, Richard P. Herden and Frank E. Kuzmits. **Motivating Employees.** Dow Jones-Irwin, 1984.

Describes the "what and how" of motivation, and shows how to use job enrichment techniques. Includes case studies and self-assessment materials. Concise and full of practical advice, like the other booklets in the publisher's "Improving Supervisor Productivity" series.

Weiss, W. H. **Supervisor's Standard Reference Handbook.** 2nd Edition. Prentice Hall, 1988.

Guides the reader through the problems that supervisors face every day. Treats a variety of motivational challenges. Shows how to deal with these situations, and describes the techniques and approaches that have worked for supervisors in all sorts of organizations.